This book is dedicated to the most important women of my life.

My wife, Andrea
My sister, Ellen
My mother-in-law, Suzanne
My mother, Barbara

Each of these four women are so special to me in their own unique ways. First, to Andrea, my wife of over 23 years, you have given me unconditional love, support, friendship, and three of the best children a man could ask for. By being the center, our family rock, you have sacrificed so much for me, and that's the main reason I've been able to accomplish anything. As my father has said so many times, "you're the best!" I will love you forever. To my sister Ellen, whose friendship and love goes back the longest. You continue to surprise me (sometimes more shocking than surprising). Our lives would not be full without you. You always bring a smile to the face of the person you are speaking to and that's an amazing quality. To Suzanne, "the apple didn't fall far" and I can never thank you enough for that! What other babysitter calls you every weekend asking to babysit? I couldn't have dreamed of a better mother-in-law. Lastly, to my mom who was taken from us too early but left us all better off having known, loved, laughed, and lived with us all.

Table of Contents

Introduction: The Challenge!

Law #1 – Garbage In, Garbage Out

Law #2 – The Power of Your Mind

Law #3 – Being Positive vs. Being Negative

Law #4 – Change is Not a Four Letter Word

Law #5 – Loyalty is a Two Way Street

Law #6 – Accessibility Can Be a Killer

Law #7 – What Goes Around, Comes Around

Law #8 – Hard Work, Works

Law #9 – Short cuts are Longer

Law #10 – There is Strength in Numbers

Law #11 – The Good Old Days Weren't All Good

Law #12 – Better, Not Easier

Law #13 – Slow Down Life, It Lasts Longer

Law #14 – Save Your Money for a Better Life

Law #15 – Happy Wife = Happy Life

Law #16 – Healthy Lifestyle Will Help You Last

Law #17 – Exciting Things Make You More Interesting

Law #18 – Complainers Lose

Law #19 – You Need to Laugh and Smile More

Law #20 – Be the Bigger Person

Law #21 – The Ten Commandments Weren't Optional

Law #22 – Kids Spell Love as "T-I-M-E"

Law #23 – Taking Responsibility for Your Own Actions

Law #24 – "Try" and "Can't" Don't Exist

Law #25 – Life is Continued Education

Law #26 – Bad Things Happen to Good People

Table of Contents cont.

Law #27 – Would You Rather Be Right and Fail?

Law #28 – The Giver Always Feels Better and Ends Up Ahead

Law #29 – You'll Never Hit a Goal You Never Set

Law #30 – You're Not Entitled to Anything

Law #31 – It's Always Better if They Tell You

Law #32 – Extraordinary Results from Ordinary People

Law #33 – Have Passion for What You Do

Law #34 – Multi-Tasking is for Potheads & Drunks

Law #35 – People Really Like to be Complimented

Law #36 – Confidence is King

Law #37 – Slow-Walkers are Slow-Workers

Law #38 – Writing Things Down is Smart

Law #39 – Never Give Up!

Law #40 – Never Hesitate to say, "I Love You"

Law #41 – Death is Inevitable

Law #42 – Finish Strong

Wrap Up: How to Learn More

Introduction: The Challenge!

These laws were learned over my 50 years, first from my mom and dad, then my brothers and sister, then my friends, then my basketball coaches, then my wife, then my father-in-law, then my mother-in-law, then my business contacts (employees, franchisees, etc.), then my kids, then my pastor's, then the many seminars I've been to and books I've read.

This book was written in short, "note taking" style. It's as if you went to an incredible number of seminars or read a large volume of books in many different categories and I'm giving you the notes to study. The idea is to use these "laws" many times over many years. My hope is that by referring back to these often, they will become second nature to you and your children.

Law #1
Garbage In, Garbage Out

- Works with computers. Why would you think it wouldn't work with your brain?

- 90% of all the media is negative, so I try to eliminate the negatives in my life, especially in the morning. Don't read the newspaper in the morning or watch TV news. It will bring you down!

- Where you go, like strip clubs or night clubs, can be very embarrassing if someone else knew. You need to stop – it's a reflection of you.

- Is internet pornography affecting you? Stop it.

- Stay away from this garbage. It will lead you down terrible paths.

- Use this simple measure: If you're embarrassed by it, stop it.

Law #2
The Power of Your Mind

- It can cure diseases: cancer, tumors, sickness.

- If you believe, it can be!

- There is such powerful energy from people that truly believe they will succeed, that they usually do!

- You must think of what you want to accomplish or look like and picture yourself more successful than you are today!

- You've heard of athletes that reporters say, "willed the team to victory."

- "Refuse to Lose," and losing won't be an option!

Law #3
Be Positive vs. Being Negative

- Find the good in everything – it's there, you just have to find it.
- Half full or half empty? How do you see things?
- In almost everything we do, it's truly a battle between the positive people who think they can and the negative people who always think you can't!
- Attitude is everything. A positive attitude will make up for a lot of other deficiencies.

Law #4
Change is Not a Four Letter Word

- In order to improve, something must change.
- You must accept and embrace change.
- The time to change is before you have to.
- We live in a changing time, so don't ever be a dinosaur and become extinct!
- We always say at our company, "The definition of insanity is doing the same thing over and over and expecting different results."
- "Change is good" (repeat that often)

Law #5
Loyalty is a Two Way Street

- If you want people to be loyal, you must be loyal yourself.
- Loyalty is always earned.
- Being loyal does not mean ignoring deficiencies or lack of production.
- Your first loyalty should be to your wife or husband.
- My mother-in-law is the most loyal individual I've ever met and it can be such an endearing quality.
- Loyalty can also stop you from making aggressive decisions in business – for good and bad!

Law #6
Accessibility can be a Killer

- Cell Phone/ Pagers/ Text Messaging – are you always accessible?
- You are helping everyone else get what they want done when they want it done and they are stealing your time away from you, which makes it harder for you to accomplish your goals.
- By the way, I don't care when you go to the bathroom so take it off Facebook! (Journals and diaries were made to be private).
- Having cell phones go off in meetings or constantly text messaging while you are with someone else is rude.
- Why is the conversation from your phone (text) more important than the one you are currently having?
- Technological advances are great, but must be controlled.

Law #7
What Goes Around, Comes Around

- Volunteer your time in a church or school.

- Give to charities or help them out.

- If you take advantage of someone, eventually someone will take advantage of you.

- Help out others – Treat everyone the way you would like to be treated.

- Help others achieve their goals and then they will help you.

- Don't take credit for the achievements of others.

Law #8
Hard Work, Works

- Usually if you work harder, good things will come.

- When you work harder than others, it builds your confidence to succeed. The team that practices harder has an advantage.

- There is more satisfaction in accomplishments that are truly earned, than things given.

- As a young business person, I learned early that I didn't have the experience or talent, but I could out work everyone. That was easy. Come in early, stay late. As we say, "Do whatever it takes!"

- Laziness is a "Dream Killer". It will kill every dream you ever have.

Law #9
Shortcuts are Longer

- Stop wasting time always looking for shortcuts.
- The time you're spending looking for a shortcut could be used to accomplish anything.
- Skipping steps and cutting corners lead to missing important items down the road.
- Always remember if it looks shorter, it's probably longer.

Law #10
There is Strength in Numbers

- Good family and friends – more is better!
- Bad friends and family can be a huge negative impact on you and your family. Lose bad friend's phone numbers if they won't change.
- More mentors, more answers and advice.
- More referrals, more business.
- Put all the numbers in life in your favor.
- Casinos were built with all of the money from people that lost at games that are in the casinos favor.

Law #11
The Good Old Days Weren't All Good

- My definition of someone being old is not a number. It's if they spend more time talking about the past than talking about the future or what they want to accomplish.

- "Really old" is if you can't remember the past to talk about!

- The same people that talk about the "good old days" forget they had no TV remote to change channels and had to get up from the couch and change channels.

- No internet or cell phones to communicate with loved ones.

- Our older generations need to be reminded of all the conveniences they enjoy today, due to our advancements and superior technology.

- There were great times in your past and challenges you overcame. No different than today. Having memories is fantastic. Constantly wishing for you to go back in time is wrong and delusional.

Law #12
Better, Not Easier

- Do things the best way, not always the easiest way.

- One time I was with an owner out cold calling and we came across a dentist office. The owner wanted to skip it because the dentist wouldn't have any need for signs, but I refused to skip it and dragged him in. After hearing my "pitch" the receptionist told us they had no need at which time the owner gave me the biggest, "I told you so" look imaginable. As we walked out, a patient waiting in the lobby said, "Did you say signs?" and I said, "Yes!" He went on to say he ran the largest construction company in the area and was not happy with his sign company. At that time, I gave that owner his "I told you so" look right back! Today, that company is still one of his largest accounts and we would not have gotten it if we didn't go into the dentist office. Better is not always easier.

- Cold calling is not the easiest way to get customers, but it's the best way. Face to face is better than mail, email, or the phone.

Law #13
Slow Down Life, It Lasts Longer

- Mick Jagger sang in a song, "Time is on your side" and then he said, "Yes, it is". Well, no it isn't.
- Life is flying by us all and we must slow it down. (Don't just look ahead to one thing, learn to plug other things in your schedule.)
- Talk about other things, not just the one big thing (vacation, holiday, etc.) It's called the "precious present". You need to be in the moment!
- Learn to appreciate the special moments and little things.
- Stop what you're doing and really listen.

Law #14
Save Your Money for a Better Life

- Money helps you buy what you want, when you want it.
- More sacrifice + less debt = less stress.
- Money gives you more independence.
- Money is not bad, just don't worship it! (It's the dirtiest god anyone could have).
- Saving money is a mindset. It should be done every month of your life, even if you just save $50 a month. Just do it.
- My dad would ask, "Do you hate money?" when he felt we were ignoring opportunities, or not saving properly.

Law #15
Happy Wife = Happy Life

- Bob Schuemann of "The Gathering" always says this and boy is he right. Coach is one of the most special people I've ever met. His organization is one of my favorites. A group that focuses on men, and improving our world through Jesus Christ.

- Go for walks with your spouse.

- Have a date night as often as you can, at least once a week.

- Remember, "If momma ain't happy, no one else will be."

- Your kids will look at the way you treat each other. The key is what Aretha Franklin sang about, "R-E-S-P-E-C-T". In order to get it, you must give it first.

Law #16
Healthy Lifestyle Will Help You Last

- Drink more water every day (8+ glasses a day).

- Exercise more – at least 3 – 5 times a week.

- Eat better food – no fast food or fried food.

- More vegetables and fruits, chicken and fish.

- No smoking (quit or never start).

- Keep alcohol in moderation.

- Moderation and portion control is something my wife has been stressing for years and she's right.

- Get at least 6 to 8 hours of sleep each night.

- Take care of yourself, so you can take care of everything else!

Law #17
Exciting Things Make You More Interesting

- Trips to faraway places for vacations.
- Go on a mission trip.
- Accomplishments – a marathon, a new business
- Go to concerts, games, or special events.
- Life is made for living! So, live it!
- Stop watching life on TV – Go live it! (Reality TV is for losers)

Law #18
Complainers Lose

- They lose time and energy.
- They lose business, employees and opportunities.
- They make everyone around them negative.
- They lose friends.
- I really make an effort not to hate, but I do hate complainers.
- As an old employee used to say, "stop your wanking!" – Stop complaining.
- The time and effort it takes to complain could be spent accomplishing the task or goal!

Law #19
You Need to Laugh and Smile More

- Everyday, make it fun to be with you! We have a long-term employee named Tony Foley and he lives by this principal. He accomplishes a lot, but he is always laughing or making someone laugh. It's contagious.
- Smiling and laughing is contagious to everyone around you.
- Studies show people that laugh and smile more, live longer.
- Now go find a nice, clean joke and tell someone.
- I love practical jokes and recently I pulled a good one on some friends. There is no doubt they will get me back – but there is also no doubt it has made us closer friends! Boy, did we all have a great laugh.
- My sister, Ellen, can always make you laugh and smile. What a great way to live.

Law #20
Be the Bigger Person

- People will make mistakes – so will you.
- Forgiveness sets you free from revenge!
- In today's culture, people always need someone to blame for anything bad that happens to them. As Southwest Airlines says about overhead luggage, "Be careful, because shift happens."
- Everyone is so into suing people that make mistakes. They do it for their own personal gain and they lose sight of what is right or any sense of fairness.
- Accept apologies and move on with life.

Law #21
The Ten Commandments Weren't Optional

- It would help if you read them and knew them all.
- Living by them is not hard.
- I am the Lord your God. You shall have no other gods before me.
- You shall not make for yourself an idol.
- You shall not make wrongful use of the name of your God.
- Remember the Sabbath and keep it holy.
- Honor your father and mother.
- You shall not murder.
- You shall not commit adultery.
- You shall not steal.
- You shall not bear false witness against your neighbor.
- You shall not covet your neighbor's wife. You shall not covet anything that belongs to your neighbor.
- It is hard to live by these, if you don't know them!

Law #22
Kids Spell Love as "T-I-M-E"

- Josh McDowell said this at a seminar my wife and I attended and I'll never forget it.

- Kids will always look around to see if you are there, for anything, so be there.

- What you value most, is reflected to others, by the time you put into it.

- "The List" is something I came up with to teach my kids things that I felt they needed. We spent time each morning on it driving to school. Each day I would work with them until they each memorized the whole thing. Here it is:

The List

For A.J., Austin and Andrew

- HONESTY – Always tell the truth
- HARDWORK – Work harder than the others
- RESPECT – Respect other people
- DEDICATION – Dedicate yourself to good
- PRACTICE – Practice Everyday
- BE ON TIME, LOMBARDI TIME – You have to be 10 minutes early
- KEEP PROMISES – Because a Promise is a Promise
- COMPLIMENT OTHERS – Say good things about other people
- SMILE AND BE HAPPY & THANKFUL FOR ALL YOU HAVE
- BE POSITIVE – Don't complain. POSITIVE is Good and NEGATIVE is Bad.
- BE PROUD OF YOURSELF AND FAMILY
- LOVE GOD – Go to Church each Sunday
- BE HEALTHY – Exercise each day
- BE FORGIVING – If somebody does something bad to you, you have to forgive them.
- IT'S BETTER TO GIVE THAN TO GET
- LOOK PEOPLE IN THE EYES AND SPEAK UP
- ALWAYS WATCH OUT FOR YOUR BROTHERS
- PLEASE AND THANK YOU

Law #23
Taking Responsibility for Your Own Actions

- "If it's to be, it's up to me." Say it out loud!

- Stop blaming others for your problems.

- One of the biggest problems in our society today is that many people do not take responsibility for their own actions (babies, child support, divorce, robbery, etc…)

- Always remember if you're pointing a finger at someone, there are 3 other fingers pointing at you!

- Get in the habit of looking in the mirror before blaming someone else.

Law #24
"Try" and "Can't" Don't Exist

- Don't try – do it.

- Stop with the "can't" – Yes you can!

- My father's opinion of "try" and "can't" was that they were the worst words to use. He would prefer many four lettered curse words to these!

- These are excuse words for you not to accomplish something.

- Eliminate these words from your vocabulary.

Law #25
Life is Continued Education

- Read more books

- Go to seminars

- Always strive to improve and learn from others.

- The moment you think you are a "finished" product, you are finished.

- Education is a lifelong journey.

- No one better epitomizes this than my father-in-law, as he says, "He's 75 years young." If he's always looking to learn and grow at his age, why shouldn't we all?

- If you could learn from other people's mistakes, and not have to go through the pain or loss yourself, why wouldn't you?

Law #26
Bad Things Happen to Good People

- It's not what happens to you that matters, it's how you handle what happens to you.

- All of us will have terrible things happen.

- Bitter or Better? You always have a choice.

- "Victims never win" – so don't play the victim role.

- When I was in the 5th grade, I took the test to see if I was color blind and failed! Within all those dots of color, I couldn't see what the nurse was asking me to find. She then went on to tell me I could never be a pilot. I was devastated and cried until my mother came to pick me up from school. When she saw me, she asked, "What's wrong, Ray?" I told her what the nurse said, and that I couldn't be a pilot. My mother said, "That's ok. You didn't want to be a pilot anyway!" She was right! I wiped my eyes and went to the courts to play basketball.

- Life is not fair so stop trying to rationalize things. Accept it and move on.

- Lastly, don't blame God when something bad happens. Some people take all the credit for the good things and blame God for the bad things. Some things we're not capable of understanding, so stop trying to figure them out. God is good, but bad things still happen.

Law #27
Would You Rather Be Right and Fail?

- Some people would rather be right and have something bad happen, then be proven wrong and have something good happen.

- Egos will make us all do things we wouldn't if we took a step back and looked at it again.

- Don't be like Fonzi in the old "Happy Days" show. He always had trouble saying the word, "wrong". He would say, "wra, wra, wra". It's always great when someone starts off by saying, "I was wrong" or "sorry about that – I was wrong." I always seem to believe and trust those people more.

- Some people are just so stubborn, they refuse to succeed!

- When we would make mistakes on the basketball court, we would say, "my bad" and then just play on. Now that would be a great way to live life.

Law #28
The Giver Always Feels Better and Ends Up Ahead

- Give money to charities that "move" you.
- Give your time to good causes.
- Mentor someone – Job Shadow Program.
- By giving, you always get more back.
- Send someone a surprise card or gift. You will be amazed at how much they will like the smallest book or special note!
- I've always enjoyed giving gifts more than receiving them.

Law #29
You'll Never Hit a Goal You Never Set

- Set high goals every year.
- Write them down – short term and long term.
- Post them up so others will see them. Maybe they'll hold you accountable to achieve them!
- Have an action plan to accomplish each of them.
- Review the goals during the year and adjust them as needed.
- It's ok to be unrealistic as long as you know it. So, as they say, "If you shoot for the moon you may end up hitting the stars."
- Don't have 50 goals. Choose 5 good ones each year and accomplish them.
- A thirty year old that does this for 20 years will accomplish 100 of their goals!

Law #30
You're Not Entitled to Anything

- The feeling of entitlement in this country is really out of control.

- Do it the old fashion way and "earn it".

- You get a much higher level of satisfaction when you truly accomplish things and get rewarded for doing it.

- All little leaguers are not "winners" just for participating. Trophies and awards for just showing up? Not keeping score? Losing makes winning down the road that much better!

- Almost 50% of our country doesn't pay taxes and are given things from our government. The top 10% income earners pay 70% of all the taxes. Which group would you rather belong to? I'd rather be in the top 10%! Go out and make a difference. Don't wait for someone to give you things.

Law #31
It's Always Better if They Tell You

- Be humble about your accomplishments.

- Satchel Paige used to say, "It ain't bragging if you did it." Well sorry Satchel, but it is bragging.

- You never need to remind people of how good you are, or of what great deeds you've done. If you do, it will always take away from you or the accomplishment.

- Go give something to a charity anonymously and don't tell anyone.

- Go out and win an award without nominating yourself.

Law #32
Extraordinary Results from Ordinary People?

- Jim Valvano, the great coach at North Carolina State said, "I once saw a great Olympian speak that said that life is made up of a bunch of ordinary people, accomplishing extraordinary results. Well, no one's more ordinary than me." He went on to win the NCAA's and was the reason behind the V Foundation to find a cure for cancer, before he passed away from cancer.

- How does this happen? Drive. The people that want it more usually get it – whatever it is!

- An old coach of mine used to say, "How bad do you wanna be good?" Pay the price and win the prize.

- I'm an ordinary guy that has accomplished some extraordinary things, by the grace of God and some great people. I've climbed the Harbor Bridge in Sydney, been on the Great Wall of China, been to Robbins Island, South Africa (Nelson Mandela's prison), built a worldwide business, met the President in the Oval Office, been the best father and husband I could be (always room to improve), and I'm a lifelong "B" student with an average intellect. Ordinary people accomplishing extraordinary results. Join the club!

Law #33
Have Passion for What You Do

- "Do what you love and love what you do" is often quoted to college students graduating.

- If you can't get excited about it, it better lead to something you will be excited about.

- This could be work, family, your relationships, your health, etc. Have a passion for it and watch how far it will take you.

- Through my children's school, I have become friendly with a former graduate, Heath Evans. Heath played in the NFL for the Seahawks, Patriots, Dolphins and Saints. Most people think his talent propelled him to the NFL. It didn't. Not that he's not talented, he is. It was his drive and passion that lead him into the NFL. Even more admirable is his passion for Jesus in all he does!

- To me, if I was picking two ingredients for success, mine would be: hard work and passion. It's that important.

- People with passion are more enthusiastic and that helps them accomplish more things.

- People with passion attract other successful people that want more of "that" in their lives.

Law #34
Multi-Tasking is for Potheads & Drunks

- Did you know that according to Jim Collins, author of Good to Great, people that multi-task (do emails while on the phone) have so diminished their brain that it is equal to someone stoned? You're doing two things, but neither one really well.

- Focus on the person/ project at hand and do it well.

- By doing too many things at once you are watering down yourself.

- Texting while driving a car is worse than driving with twice the legal amount of alcohol in your system! No, I'm not saying it's better to drink and drive than texting while driving. They are both bad.

- Now just go do one thing really well, then the next, and the next!

Law #35
People Really Like to be Complimented

- Catch people doing good things and tell them.

- Stop taking family and friends for granted. Tell them how you feel about them.

- Throw out compliments about hair, dress, kids – anything that is sincere will be well received.

- You read really well! (Thanks for reading this book.) Did you smile or laugh? That's how easy it is to make people feel better.

Law #36
Confidence is King

- Nobody will follow an unsure leader.

- I used to have a coach that said, "I want all of you to be confident, bordering on cockiness." It's a fine line that you have to check to make sure you don't cross that line.

- Being confident is a mind-set for almost all things you do and want to accomplish.

- Your body language says a lot about how confident you are about anything.

- Look 'em in the eyes. Stand up tall. Let everyone see that you are confident and will get it done. Then, go get it done!

Law #37
Slow-Walkers are Slow-Workers

- This sounds crazy, but it's not. Show me a slow walker and they are usually a slow worker.

- I want people that walk quick and work quick.

- Pace matters – Faster usually wins.

- It's better to get more done and make some mistakes, than get 1 or 2 things done.

- I'm not saying be sloppy or don't do anything perfect, but you have to move at a fast pace if you want success.

Law #38
Writing Things Down is Smart

- Taking notes takes the pressure off of your memory.

- Have a pad and pen next to your bed and use it to write anything down that is stopping you from sleeping.

- I always hate it when a waiter or waitress takes a big order from a group without writing it down. Inevitably they come back and ask questions or worse, get the order wrong.

- Note taking also is a form of a compliment in business. Meaning, you are telling the other person that what they are saying is important enough for you to write it down! When you interview for a job, ask questions and take notes.

Law #39
Never Give Up!

- Most failures wouldn't happen if people didn't quit.

- Quitters never win and winners never quit.

- Sometimes you have to change or stop doing something the same way – but never give up.

- As I've raised my kids, they know very well that we don't quit. We never give up.

- We may fail, make mistakes, and disappoint each other, but we never give up!

Law #40
Never Hesitate to say, "I Love You"

- I tell my wife and kids, every chance I get. (Every day).

- Growing up we were not an "I love you" type of family. It was something I think we all just assumed. This was not good and I have changed this with my family.

- Don't take your loved ones for granted – tell them every day.

- I would never want my loved ones to ever question or doubt my love for them.

Law #41
Death is Inevitable

- No matter your circumstances or what you have done death will come.

- Accept Jesus as your Lord and Savior and it will set you free.

- No more worry, put your faith in Jesus.

- Reading the bible and praying works to help eliminate some anxiety about death, but accepting Jesus is the only way to get to Heaven.

- I used to look at death as such a horrible thing. Today, I realize that without death, life would not be as highly valued.

- Jesus died for our sins. The least you could do is recognize it and spread the good news.

Law #42
Finish Strong

- What you start, you must finish.

- In life, having a good idea and working it is only a part of success. Finishing is what it's all about!

- I used to have a basketball coach that said, "Making a great move and missing the lay-up is like going to the restroom, opening your zipper and peeing in your pants. It makes no sense at all." Well, that's a little rough, but you get the idea. Finish the job. Make the layup.

- Are you striving to hear the words from our heavenly father, "Well done, my good and faithful servant"? Now that's finishing strong!

I hope you've enjoyed these "laws" and put them to good use in your everyday life. One of my goals before I leave this world is to be a huge positive influence on as many people as possible. My prayer is that now you are one of them!

~The End~

Wrap up: To Learn More

I hope you have found these "laws" to be an easy way to learn and improve as a human being. My prayer is that you continue to grow and fully become the person God intended you to be. Thank you for taking the time to read this book.

To learn more and take the next step:
Please visit www.lawsofinevitability.com.

Some great charities, schools, and churches to consider giving to:

The King's Academy
The King's Academy is a private, nonprofit, college preparatory, interdenominational Christian school.
www.tka.net
561-686-4244

Family Church of West Palm Beach
A church family that believes in the Bible as the absolute truth and God's final authority. Attendees at Family Church are taught to seek and follow the truth of God's work by living it in their everyday lives.
www.gofamilychurch.org
561-650-7400

Junior Achievement
Junior Achievement (JA) empowers young people to own their economic success. Their volunteer-delivered, K-12 programs foster work-readiness, entrepreneurship and financial literacy skills, and use experiential learning to inspire kids to dream big and reach their potential. Junior Achievement impacts 4 million U.S. students in more than 176,000 classrooms.
www.ja.org
719-540-8000

Habitat for Humanity
A global nonprofit Christian housing organization that seeks to put God's love into action by bringing people together to build homes, communities and hope. Since 1976, Habitat has served more than 500,000 families by welcoming people of all races, religions and nationalities to construct, rehabilitate or preserve homes; by advocating for fair and just housing policies; and by providing training and access to resources to help families improve their shelter conditions.
www.habitat.org
1-800-HABITAT

The Gathering
The Gathering USA is a ministry of evangelism, discipleship and mission opportunities for men.
www.thegatheringpb.com
561-622-4913

Made in the USA
Columbia, SC
21 August 2024

40913933R00021